BENIN 2016 HUMAN RIGHTS REPORT

EXECUTIVE SUMMARY

Benin is a stable constitutional parliamentary democracy (republic). On March 20, voters elected Patrice Talon to a five-year term in a multiparty election, replacing former president Thomas Boni Yayi, who served two consecutive five-year terms. In April 2015 authorities held legislative elections in which former president Yayi's supporting coalition, Cowry Force for an Emerging Benin, won 33 of 83 seats in the National Assembly, and the coalition allied with four independent candidates held 37 seats (a decrease from 41 in the prior legislature). International observers viewed both the March presidential and 2015 legislative elections as generally free, fair, and transparent.

Civilian authorities generally maintained effective control over the security forces.

The major human rights problems included police use of excessive force, harsh prison conditions, and vigilante violence.

Other human rights problems included: arbitrary arrest and detention; prolonged pretrial detention; abuse of women and children, including sexual harassment, child sexual exploitation, early and forced marriage, and infanticide; trafficking in persons; discrimination against persons with disabilities; violence and discrimination against women and girls, including female genital mutilation/cutting (FGM/C); and child labor.

Impunity was a problem. Although the government made an effort to control corruption and abuses, including by prosecuting and punishing public officials, officials sometimes engaged in corrupt practices with impunity.

Section 1. Respect for the Integrity of the Person, Including Freedom from:

a. Arbitrary Deprivation of Life and other Unlawful or Politically Motivated Killings

There were several reports the government or its agents committed arbitrary or unlawful killings, claiming self-defense.

On April 5, a police officer shot and killed Latifa Boukari in the city of Bassila (northwest Benin) following a complaint filed by an individual to whom Boukari allegedly owed CFA francs 30,000 ($51). Police stated that Boukari was resisting arrest when the officer shot him. In reaction to the killing, local residents burned alive the individual who filed the complaint with police. The police officer who killed Boukari reportedly fled Bassila following the killing.

On January 6, a sentry shot and killed Corporal Mohamed Dangou during an attempt to detain him for questioning at the Guezo military camp in Cotonou. Authorities stated that in December 2015 Dangou and four other peacekeeping troops serving in Cote d'Ivoire masterminded protests regarding the government's withholding of bonus payment to its peacekeeping troops there. Chief of defense staff, General Awal Nagnimi, claimed in a press conference after the shooting that Dangou refused to be taken in for questioning by gendarmes, and the sentry posted at the entrance of the military camp shot Dangou while he tried to flee the camp. On April 22, Alfred Hamelo, the sentry who shot Dangou, was placed under court supervision (controle judicaire). On July 28, the Constitutional Court ruled that the military had violated article eight of the constitution related to the inviolability of the human person and, as an instrument of the state, its obligation to respect and protect that person. The court also ordered reparations for the violation.

b. Disappearance

There were no reports of politically motivated disappearances.

c. Torture and Other Cruel, Inhuman, or Degrading Treatment or Punishment

The constitution and law prohibit such practices, but such incidents occurred.

On April 28, the Constitutional Court ruled that the acting director of the Prison of Cotonou, Lieutenant Bariou Fatoumbi, violated article 18 of the constitution related to torture and other cruel, inhuman, or degrading treatment. The court decision was based on evidence that Lieutenant Fatoumbi ordered a sick female prisoner handcuffed and chained to a bed for 12 days at the Teaching Hospital of Cotonou.

The United Nations reported that as of December 20, it received two allegations of sexual exploitation and abuse against Beninese peacekeepers. An allegation involving military personnel deployed to the UN Multidimensional Integrated Stabilization Mission in Mali was under Beninese government investigation at year's end. An allegation regarding a 2015 incident involving Beninese UN police in Haiti was found to be unsubstantiated.

Prison and Detention Center Conditions

Prison conditions were harsh and life threatening due to inadequate food, overcrowding, and inadequate sanitary conditions and medical care.

<u>Physical Conditions</u>: Overcrowding and lack of proper sanitation, potable water, and medical facilities posed risks to prisoners' health. The 2015 Watchdog on the Justice System in Benin report stated that conditions in the country's 10 civil prisons were inhuman, with overcrowding, malnutrition, and disease common. Nine of the 10 civil prisons were filled far beyond capacity. There were deaths due to lack of medical care, neglect, and poor ventilation in cramped and overcrowded cells. Lighting was inadequate. Prisoners with mental disabilities lacked access to appropriate disability-related support and services. According to the 2015 report, prison authorities forced prisoners to pay "bed taxes" for spaces to sleep and made sick prisoners in the civil prison of Cotonou pay to visit the hospital.

On April 27, inmates at the Civil Prison of Abomey (in central Benin) staged a violent protest regarding harsh prison conditions, especially a weeklong lack of drinking water in the prison.

Prison overcrowding was a serious problem. According to the nongovernmental organization (NGO) Watchdog on the Justice System in Benin the prison population (including pretrial detainees, remand prisoners, and convicts) in 2015 totaled 5,820. Pretrial detainees and remanded prisoners represented 75 percent of the total prison population. These numbers did not include detainees held in police stations and in civilian and military detention centers. According to 2012 statistics from the International Center for Prison Studies, female prisoners constituted 5 percent of the prison population and juveniles 2 percent.

Authorities housed juveniles at times with adults and held pretrial detainees with convicted prisoners, although not with the most violent convicts.

<u>Administration</u>: Authorities did not use alternatives to incarceration for nonviolent offenders. There was no formal system to submit complaints without censorship to judicial authorities. According to the 2015 Watchdog on the Justice System in Benin Authorities report, prison authorities charged visitors amounts ranging from 500 CFA francs to 1,000 CFA francs (approximately $1 to $2).

<u>Independent Monitoring</u>: The government permitted prison visits by human rights monitors. Religious groups and NGOs visited prisons, although some NGOs complained credentials were not systematically granted when they submitted requests to make visits. Organizations that visited prisons included the local chapter of Prison Fellowship, Caritas, Prisons Brotherhood, Christian Action for the Abolition of Torture, the French Development Agency, Rotaract (Rotary International), and Prisoners without Borders.

<u>Improvements</u>: On June 16, the National Assembly passed a law to reduce prison overcrowding that provides for community service in lieu of prison sentences for first-time offenders convicted of minor offenses.

d. Arbitrary Arrest or Detention

The constitution and law prohibit arbitrary arrest and detention; however, security forces occasionally failed to observe these prohibitions.

Role of the Police and Security Apparatus

Police, under the Ministry of Interior, have primary responsibility for enforcing law and maintaining order in urban areas; the gendarmerie, under the Ministry of Defense, performs the same functions in rural areas.

Police were inadequately equipped and poorly trained. The government responded to these problems by building more stations and modernizing equipment; however, problems remained.

Impunity was a problem. Police leadership often did not punish and sometimes protected officers who committed abuses, which led to the president's personal involvement in the resolution of several cases of security force abuses. Individuals may file complaints of police abuse with the police leadership, the lower courts, the mediator of the republic (ombudsman), or the Constitutional Court. The inspector general of the National Police Investigation Division is responsible for investigating serious, sensitive, and complex cases involving police personnel. The mandate of the Investigation Division is to conduct administrative and judiciary investigations involving police and to advise the director of national police on disciplinary action.

On October 25, the Office of the President issued a statement in response to repeated complaints of police officers extorting money during security checks. The president announced the opening of telephone and internet hotlines for citizens to denounce such cases.

Military disciplinary councils deal with minor offenses committed by members of the military. The councils have no jurisdiction over civilians. The country has no military tribunal, so civilian courts deal with serious crimes involving the gendarmerie and the military.

Arrest Procedures and Treatment of Detainees

The constitution requires arrest warrants based on sufficient evidence and issued by a duly authorized judicial official, and requires a hearing before a magistrate within 48 hours, but this requirement was not always observed. After examining a detainee, the judge has 24 hours to decide whether to continue to detain or release the individual. Under exceptional circumstances, or in arrests involving illegal drugs including narcotics, the judge may authorize detention beyond 72 hours but not to exceed an additional eight days. Warrants authorizing pretrial detention are effective for six months and may be renewed every six months until a suspect is brought to trial. Detainees have the right to prompt judicial determination of the legality of detention, which was generally observed. Detainees were promptly informed of charges against them. Detainees awaiting judicial decisions may request release on bail; however, the attorney general must agree to the request. They have the right to prompt access to a lawyer after being brought before a judge, which authorities also generally observed. They are allowed to have family visits (see section 1.c.). The government provided counsel to indigents in criminal cases. Suspects were not detained incommunicado or held under house arrest.

There were credible reports gendarmes and police often exceeded the legal limit of 48 hours of detention, sometimes by as much as a week. Authorities often held persons indefinitely "at the disposal of" the Public Prosecutor's Office before presenting the case to a magistrate.

Arbitrary Arrest: Arbitrary arrests and detentions occurred. In February 2015 a judge at the Court of Porto-Novo ordered the immediate release of a prisoner who had completed a nine-year prison term on criminal charges. The prosecutor did not authorize the prisoner's release for an additional one and one-half months. The prisoner filed a complaint with the Constitutional Court, which ruled that his continued detention violated constitutional provisions related to arbitrary detention.

<u>Pretrial Detention</u>: Approximately 75 percent of persons in prison were pretrial detainees; the length of excess pretrial detentions--any period over five years for felony cases and three years for misdemeanors--varied from two to 11 years, according to a mediator's report. Inadequate facilities, poorly trained staff, and overcrowded dockets delayed the administration of justice. The law defines the maximum length of pretrial detention for felony cases as no more than five years and for misdemeanors as no more than three years. The government often exceeded these limits. In July 2015 the Criminal Court of Cotonou sentenced a defendant accused of killing an assailant in self-defense to six months in prison after the defendant had already spent five years in detention awaiting trial. Noting the five years he had already served in pretrial detention, the court ordered his immediate release.

<u>Detainee's Ability to Challenge Lawfulness of Detention before a Court</u>: A person arrested or detained, regardless of whether on criminal or other grounds, is entitled to file a complaint with the liberty and detention chamber of the relevant court. The presiding judge may order the individual's release if determined to have been unlawfully detained.

e. Denial of Fair Public Trial

The constitution and law provide for an independent judiciary, but the government did not always respect this provision. The government names judges at the Public Prosecutor's Office, making them susceptible to government influence; however, there were no instances in which the outcome of trials appeared predetermined, and authorities respected court orders. The judicial system was also subject to corruption, although the government made substantial anticorruption efforts, including the creation in 2014 of an independent National Anti-Corruption Authority and the dismissal and arrest of government officials allegedly involved in corruption scandals.

Trial Procedures

While the constitution provides for the right to a fair trial, judicial inefficiency and corruption impeded the exercise of this right.

The legal system is based on French civil law and local customary law. A defendant is presumed innocent. Defendants enjoy the right to be informed promptly and in detail of the charges with free interpretation as necessary. A defendant has the right to be present at trial and to representation by an attorney. The court provides indigent defendants with counsel upon request in criminal cases. Government-provided counsel, however, was not always available, especially in cases handled in courts located in the north, since most lawyers lived in the south. Defendants are entitled to free interpretation services as necessary from the moment charged through all appeals. Defendants enjoy the right to adequate time and facilities to prepare a defense. A defendant has the right to confront witnesses and to have access to government-held evidence. Defendants are allowed to present witnesses and evidence on their own behalf. Defendants enjoy the right not to be compelled to testify or confess guilt. Defendants may appeal criminal convictions to the Court of Appeals and the Supreme Court, after which they may appeal to the president for a pardon. Trials are open to the public, but in exceptional circumstances the president of the court may decide to restrict access to preserve public order or to protect the parties. The government extends the above rights to all citizens without discrimination.

Political Prisoners and Detainees

There were no reports of political prisoners or detainees.

Civil Judicial Procedures and Remedies

The judiciary exercised independence in civil matters. If administrative or informal remedies are unsuccessful, a citizen may file a complaint concerning an alleged human rights violation with the Constitutional Court. The Constitutional Court's ruling is not binding on courts; citizens, however, may use rulings from the Constitutional Court to initiate legal action against offenders in regular courts. Adverse court rulings other than those of the Constitutional Court may be appealed to the Economic Community of West African States' Court of Justice and the African Court on Human and People's Rights. On February 8, the government filed a declaration with the African Union Commission recognizing the competence of the African Court on Human and Peoples' Rights to receive cases from NGOs and individuals.

f. Arbitrary or Unlawful Interference with Privacy, Family, Home, or Correspondence

The constitution and law prohibit such actions, and the government generally respected these prohibitions.

Section 2. Respect for Civil Liberties, Including:

a. Freedom of Speech and Press

The constitution provides for freedom of speech and press, and the government generally respected these rights.

There were a large number of public and private media outlets, including two public and five private television stations, one public and 50 private radio stations, and approximately 175 newspapers and periodicals. Many of these were openly critical of authorities, nearly always without consequence.

Unlike in previous years, there were few reports the government inhibited freedom of the press.

Press and Media Freedoms: The press and media were closely regulated, and the government considered itself to have an essential role in ensuring the press did not behave in an "irresponsible" or "destabilizing" way. The High Authority for Audiovisual and Communication (HAAC) is a quasi-governmental commission with members appointed by the president, private media, and the legislature. HAAC has a dual--and perhaps inherently contradictory--role of ensuring press freedom and protecting the country against inflammatory, irresponsible, or destabilizing coverage. On February 3, HAAC banned private television broadcaster Golfe TV from any political reporting, including coverage of news on the presidential election. HAAC issued this decision because Golfe TV violated a previous HAAC decree restricting media coverage of events prior to the official opening of the presidential election campaign season. On February 9, HAAC lifted the suspension following a meeting with members of the Federation of Radio and Television Employers.

On February 2, HAAC issued two decrees to grant all 33 presidential candidates equal access to state-owned and private media for publicizing their political agenda.

The government typically countered accusations of infringing on press freedom with arguments stating the need to support press freedoms while also preventing press activity that may threaten the stability of the country or willfully misinform the public. In January 2015 the government banned the reprint and distribution of an issue of the French satirical newspaper, *Charlie Hebdo*. The statement condemned the terrorist attacks that took place in France that month while simultaneously noting the government's responsibility to provide for public safety and respect of religious principles and public figures.

Independent media were active and expressed a wide variety of views without restriction. Publications criticized the government freely and frequently. A nongovernmental media ethics commission censured some journalists for unethical conduct, such as reporting falsehoods or inaccuracies or releasing information that was embargoed by the government.

The government owned and operated the most influential media organizations by controlling broadcast range and infrastructure. Private television and radio had poorer coverage due to inadequate equipment and limited broadcast ranges awarded to them by HAAC.

Most citizens were illiterate, lived in rural areas, and generally received news via radio. The state-owned National Broadcasting Company broadcast in French and in 18 local languages.

Censorship or Content Restrictions: HAAC publicly warned media outlets against publishing information related to legal cases pending before a criminal court because it could be interpreted as an attempt to influence the ruling of the court. It was possible to purchase and thus influence the content of press coverage. HAAC warned the media against such practices. Some journalists practiced self-censorship because they were indebted to government officials who granted them service contracts. Other journalists practiced self-censorship due to fear the government would suspend their media outlets. HAAC held public hearings on alleged misconduct by media outlets during the year.

Libel/Slander Laws: In January 2015, after years of lobbying by professional media associations, the National Assembly passed a revised press code, the Information and Communication Code, repealing the previous code that imposed prison sentences for conviction of certain abuses of freedom of expression. The press code, signed into law by the president in March 2015, disallows prison sentences for journalists charged with defamation and some other offenses. Although journalists may no longer be imprisoned for libel and slander, they may face legal prosecution and fines for incitement of crimes through the press.

In January 2015, prior to the enactment of the code, a broadcast journalist from the state-owned television station (ORTB) criticized a decision by the president to participate in a march in Paris against terrorism. He also called on the president to allow freedom of the press and political debates within public media. He was later suspended from doing live programs. Professional media associations, NGOs, and ethics groups denounced the measure as retaliatory. In response to trade union and NGO demonstrations, the ORTB director claimed the removal of the journalist was consistent with internal office regulations but then reinstated the television journalist.

Internet Freedom

The government did not restrict or disrupt access to the internet or censor online content, and there were no credible reports the government monitored private online communications without appropriate legal authority. According to the International Telecommunication Union, 6.8 percent of the population used the internet in 2015.

Academic Freedom and Cultural Events

There were no government restrictions on academic freedom or cultural events.

b. Freedom of Peaceful Assembly and Association

The constitution and law provide for the freedoms of assembly and association. Permits are required for demonstrations and other public gatherings. The government generally respected these rights. Although opposition groups cited instances in which they did not seek permits, anticipating they would be opposed, there were no instances of denial on political grounds.

Freedom of Assembly

The constitution and law provide for freedom of assembly, and the government generally respected this right.

The government requires and generally granted permits for use of public places for demonstrations. Authorities sometimes cited "public order" to deny requests for permits from opposition groups, civil society organizations, and labor unions.

On July 12, security forces disbanded a peaceful demonstration to demand the replacement of obsolete medical equipment staged by health-care staff of the Abomey Hospital (central Benin). The mayor of Abomey declared the demonstration a "threat to public order."

c. Freedom of Religion

See the Department of State's *International Religious Freedom Report* at www.state.gov/religiousfreedomreport/.

d. Freedom of Movement, Internally Displaced Persons, Protection of Refugees, and Stateless Persons

The constitution and law provide for freedom of internal movement, foreign travel, emigration, and repatriation, and the government generally respected these rights.

The government cooperated with the Office of the UN High Commissioner for Refugees (UNHCR) and other humanitarian organizations in assisting refugees and asylum seekers.

In-country Movement: The presence of police, gendarmes, and illegal roadblocks inconvenienced domestic movement. Authorities justified roadblocks as a means of enforcing vehicle safety and customs regulations, but police and gendarmes exacted bribes from travelers at many checkpoints.

Foreign Travel: The government maintained documentary requirements for minors traveling abroad as part of its continuing campaign against trafficking in persons. This was not always enforced, and trafficking of minors across borders continued.

The government's policy toward the seasonal movement of livestock allowed migratory Fulani (Peul) herdsmen from other countries to enter and depart freely; the government did not enforce designated entry points.

Protection of Refugees

Access to Asylum: The law provides for the granting of asylum or refugee status, and the government has established a system for providing protection to refugees.

Durable Solutions: The government and UNHCR assisted former refugees and asylum seekers with obtaining documents from their countries of origin while granting their status as privileged residents. The government also facilitated naturalization of refugees as part of a local integration effort. The government involved civil society, the media, and academia in the process.

The government, in partnership with UNHCR, assisted in the safe, voluntary return of three Ivorian citizens to Cote d'Ivoire during the year.

Stateless Persons

There were large communities of stateless individuals residing in eight villages along the border with Niger and Nigeria. These villages were returned to Benin following the resolution of land disputes among Benin, Niger, and Nigeria. The residents lacked the necessary identification documents to claim citizenship. During the year the Court of Natitingou, with the assistance of UNHCR, issued birth certificates to the residents of Kourou-koualou, a village along the border with Burkina Faso. In 2014, the most recent year for which information was available, the mayor of the commune of Karimama bordering Niger, informed UNHCR that there were 1,000 stateless persons in the vicinity of his commune.

Section 3. Freedom to Participate in the Political Process

The constitution and law provide citizens the ability to choose their government in free and fair periodic elections held by secret ballot and based on universal and equal suffrage.

Elections and Political Participation

Recent Elections: On March 6 and March 20, the country held the first and second rounds of the presidential election. The vote proceeded calmly and credibly despite minor technical irregularities. Local and international observers unanimously characterized the voting process as peaceful and orderly. Observers identified some delays in the provision of voting materials to polling stations and evidence of training gaps of polling agents but no anomalies that would put the fundamental integrity of the election into doubt. In April 2015 authorities conducted legislative elections to elect the 83 National Assembly members. Observers viewed the elections as generally free, fair, and transparent.

In June 2015, after more than two years of delays, long-awaited local and municipal elections took place in generally free and fair conditions despite minor irregularities and logistical challenges, including the omission on ballots of some parties and coalitions.

Participation of Women and Minorities: President Talon appointed only three female ministers to his 21-member cabinet and one woman among the prefects administering the country's 12 geographic departments. By custom and tradition, women assumed household duties, had less access to formal education, and were discouraged from involvement in politics. No laws limit the participation of women and members of minorities in the political process, and they participated. Cultural factors, however, limited women's political participation.

On June 28, human rights associations issued a joint statement to express concerns regarding the government's failure to observe gender parity in its high-ranking appointments, noting a decrease in the number of women appointed to decision-making positions in the Talon administration.

Section 4. Corruption and Lack of Transparency in Government

Although the law provides criminal penalties for corruption by officials, the government did not implement the law effectively, and officials sometimes engaged in corrupt practices with impunity. Police corruption was widespread. Police extorted money from travelers at roadblocks. It was commonly believed, and acknowledged by some judicial personnel, that the judicial system at all levels was susceptible to corruption. The World Bank's most recent Worldwide Governance Indicators reflected that corruption was a serious problem.

The government took a number of actions during the year to combat corruption, however. For example, on April 19, the National Anti-Corruption Authority (ANLC) referred three high-profile cases of corruption and other acts of economic malfeasance against the Office of Treasury and Public Accounting, the Ministry of Economy and Finance, and the National Council of Shippers to the prosecutor of the Court of Cotonou. On April 28, the authority conducted a session for court staff, gendarmes, police, civil society activists, and Ministry of Justice officials to discuss the triannual assessment of the legal procedures related to corruption and transnational organized crime.

Corruption: On July 7, the Council of Ministers acted on the findings of a commission appointed by the president that investigated fraud allegations related to the 2015 civil servant recruitment exams at the Ministry of Economy and Finance. Based on the findings, the council annulled the results of recruitment exams and excluded from future employment all the candidates found to be involved in the fraud and suspended and pursued legal action against officials involved in the fraud. In addition to 11 serving high-ranking government officials, authorities pursued legal action against former ministers of economy and finance Komi Koutche and of labor and public service Aboubacar Yaya.

Financial Disclosure: The law requires income and asset disclosure by appointed and elected public officials. Declarations are not made available to the public. On March 18, the ANLC submitted an appeal to the National Assembly urging lawmakers to submit their asset disclosure statements to the Supreme Court pursuant to Article 3 of Benin's Anti-Corruption Act. Reportedly only six out of the 83 sitting deputies in the National Assembly had submitted asset disclosure statements. At a March 6 cabinet meeting, which was publicized by the government and press, the president disclosed his assets as of the end of his term. The penalty for failure to submit an asset disclosure is a fine of six times the monthly wage of the official concerned. This penalty has never been applied.

Public Access to Information: In March 2015 the president signed into law an information and communication code that provides for increased access to government information and administrative and legal measures against government personnel who fail to grant such access. The law provides for citizen access to documents or information held by a public entity or its employees in the exercise of their duties. There are, however, several restrictions on public access to national security, trade, health, judicial, and other information deemed sensitive.

Section 5. Governmental Attitude Regarding International and Nongovernmental Investigation of Alleged Violations of Human Rights

A number of domestic and international human rights groups generally operated without government restriction, investigating and publishing their findings on human rights cases. Government officials often were cooperative and responsive to their views.

Government Human Rights Bodies: The country's ombudsman was independent, adequately resourced, and effective.

Section 6. Discrimination, Societal Abuses, and Trafficking in Persons

Women

Rape and Domestic Violence: The law prohibits rape, but enforcement was weak due to police ineffectiveness, official corruption, and victims' unwillingness to report cases due to fear of social stigma and retaliation. Prison sentences for rape convictions range from one to five years. Although the penal code does not distinguish between rapes in general and spousal rape, the 2013 Law on the

Prevention and Repression of Violence against Women explicitly prohibits spousal rape and provides the maximum penalty for conviction of raping a domestic partner. A 2011 law reinforces existing legislation against gender-based violence (GBV). In 2014 the Ministry of Labor, Civil Service, and Social Affairs' Social Promotion Centers, through the Counseling and Legal Assistance Service to GBV victims, received 12,896 cases; 83 percent of victims were girls and women and 17 percent boys. Because of the lack of police training in collecting evidence associated with sexual assaults, ignorance of the law, and inherent difficulties victims faced in preserving and presenting evidence in court, judges reduced most sexual offense charges to misdemeanors.

Penalties for conviction of domestic violence range from six to 36 months' imprisonment. Domestic violence against women was common, however. Women remained reluctant to report cases, and judges and police were reluctant to intervene in domestic disputes. The local chapter of the regional NGO Women in Law and Development-Benin (WILDAF-Benin), the Female Jurists Association of Benin, the Female Lawyers Association, and the Action Group for Justice and Social Equality offered social, legal, medical, and psychological assistance to victims of domestic violence. On April 7 and April 8, WILDAF--Benin held a session for midwives, nurses, and social workers from the northern departments on the 2013 Law on the Prevention and Repression of Violence against Women. With the assistance of an international donor, WILDAF-Benin operated one-stop care centers in Abomey and Cotonou to improve GBV victim-support services by providing legal, medical, psychosocial, and economic support to GBV victims. As of June 2015 this activity provided 470 persons with GBV services, trained 97 service providers (social workers, nurses, and midwives), and strengthened a service delivery system for GBV victims. On July 4, WILDAF-Benin launched a GBV website.

The Office of Women's Promotion under the jurisdiction of the Ministry of Labor, Civil Service, and Social Affairs is responsible for protecting and advancing women's rights and welfare.

Female Genital Mutilation/Cutting (FGM/C): The law prohibits FGM/C and provides penalties for conviction of performing the procedure, including prison sentences of up to 10 years and fines of up to six million CFA francs ($10,215). Nevertheless, FGM/C occurred, and enforcement was rare due to the code of silence associated with this crime. Individuals who were aware of an incident of FGM/C but did not report it potentially faced fines ranging from 50,000 to 100,000 CFA francs ($85 to $170). FGM/C was practiced on girls and women from infancy up to age 30, although the majority of cases occurred before age 13, with half occurring before age five. The type of FGM/C most commonly perpetrated was Type II, the total removal of the clitoris with or without the total excision of the labia minora. This practice was largely limited to remote rural areas in the north. According to the UN Children's Fund (UNICEF), 7 percent of girls and women ages 15 to 49 underwent FGM/C, and the prevalence among girls younger than 14 was 0.3 percent. The figure was higher in some regions, especially the northern departments, including Alibori and Donga (48 percent) and Borgou (59 percent), and among certain ethnic groups. More than 70 percent of Bariba and Peul (Fulani) and 53 percent of Yoa-Lokpa women and girls underwent FGM/C. Younger women were less likely to be excised than their older counterparts. Those who performed the procedure, usually older women, profited financially from it.

NGOs educated rural communities on the dangers of FGM/C and retrained FGM/C practitioners in other activities. The government, in conjunction with NGOs and international partners, made progress in raising public awareness of the dangers of the practice.

Other Harmful Traditional Practices: Forced marriage and widowhood rites, such as forcing the widow to lie beside the dead body of the deceased and to marry the deceased husband's brother (levirate), occurred in certain regions.

Sexual Harassment: The law prohibits sexual harassment and offers protection for victims, but sexual harassment was common, especially of female students by their male teachers. Persons convicted of sexual harassment face sentences of one to two years in prison and fines ranging from 100,000 to one million CFA francs ($170 to $1,702). The law also provides penalties for persons who are aware of sexual harassment and do not report it. Victims seldom reported harassment due to fear of social stigma and retaliation, however, and prosecutors and police lacked the legal knowledge and skills to pursue such cases. Although laws prohibiting sexual harassment were not widely enforced, judges used other provisions in the penal code to deal with sexual abuses involving minors.

Reproductive Rights: Couples and individuals have the right to decide the number, spacing, and timing of children, free from discrimination, coercion, or violence, but they often lacked the information and means to do so.

According to the World Health Organization, the UN Population Fund, UNICEF, and the World Bank, the maternal mortality rate was 405 deaths per 100,000 live births in 2015. Factors contributing to the high rate were deliveries without adequate medical assistance, lack of access to emergency obstetric care, and unhygienic conditions during birth. According to 2015 UN Population Fund data, only 17 percent of girls and women ages 15 to 49 used a modern method of contraception. It reported that as of 2010, 23 percent of women ages 20 to 24 had given birth before age 18. Factors influencing low contraception and early pregnancy rates included illiteracy and poor access to reproductive health information in rural areas.

Discrimination: Although the constitution provides for equality for women in political, economic, and social spheres, women experienced extensive discrimination because of societal attitudes and resistance to behavioral change. Women experienced discrimination in obtaining employment, credit, equal pay, and in owning or managing businesses (see section 7.d.).

The code of persons and the family bans all discrimination against women regarding marriage and provides for the right to equal inheritance. The nationality law, however, discriminates against women.

In rural areas women traditionally occupied a subordinate role and were responsible for much of the hard labor on subsistence farms. The government and NGOs educated the public on women's inheritance and property rights and their increased rights in marriage, including prohibitions on forced marriage, child marriage, and polygyny.

The government granted microcredit to help poor persons, especially women in rural areas, develop income-generating activities. The government extended credit and loans to female entrepreneurs.

Children

Birth Registration: Citizenship is derived by birth within the country and from the father. By law the child of a Beninese father is automatically considered a citizen, but the child of a Beninese woman is considered Beninese only if the child's father is unknown, has no known nationality, or is also Beninese. Particularly in rural areas, parents often did not declare the birth of their children, either from lack of understanding of the procedures involved or because they could not afford the fees for birth certificates. This could result in denial of public services such as education and health care.

Several donors operated programs to increase the number of registered children. For example, UNICEF supported the government's campaign to register all births and to provide birth certificates to those who did not obtain one at birth. On January 28, the Ministry of Interior organized a workshop in the city of Porto-Novo to share best practices on increasing birth registration. The workshop covered methods for increasing civil registration of births, reducing backlogs at registration centers located in major cities, and establishing offices of vital records in smaller towns and neighborhoods.

Education: Primary education was compulsory for all children between six and 11 years of age. Public school education was tuition-free for primary school students and for female students in grade nine in secondary schools, but parents often voluntarily paid tuition for their children because many schools had insufficient funds. Girls did not have the same educational opportunities as boys, and the literacy rate for women was approximately 18 percent, compared with 50 percent for men. In some parts of the country, girls received no formal education. According to UNICEF, the net primary school enrollment rate in 2011-12 was approximately 79 percent for boys and 73 percent for girls. The enrollment rate for secondary education was 53 percent for boys and 42 percent for girls.

Child Abuse: Children suffered multiple forms of abuse, including rape, sexual harassment, and abduction. The Child Code bans a wide range of harmful practices such as forced marriage, sexual abuse, FGM/C, trafficking, labor exploitation, infanticide, illegal and prolonged detention, early pregnancy, and begging. The code also sets rules for national and international adoptions, children's health care, and juvenile apprenticeships. The code provides for heavy fines and penalties with up to life imprisonment for convicted violators. The Central Office for Minors Protection in Cotonou arrested suspects and referred them to judicial authorities. In 2015 it provided temporary shelter to 820 identified victims of abuse.

Early and Forced Marriage: The law prohibits marriage under age 18 but grants exemptions for children ages 14 to 17 with parental consent and authorization of a judge. A 2014 Multiple Indicator Cluster Survey sponsored by UNICEF and the National Institute of Statistics and Economic Analysis indicated that 8.8 percent of girls and women and 1.4 percent of boys and men ages 15 to 49 were married or were cohabitating with someone of the opposite sex before age 15. The proportion of women ages 20 to 49 who were married or who were cohabitating with someone of the opposite sex before age 18 was 31.7 percent, and the proportion of men in the same age range was 6.1 percent. Early and forced marriage included barter marriage and marriage by abduction. As part of forced marriage, the groom traditionally abducts and rapes his prospective child bride. The practice was widespread in rural areas, despite government and NGO efforts to end it through information sessions on the rights of women and children. Local NGOs reported some communities concealed the practice.

In 2014 the government approved a UNICEF-sponsored National Policy of Child Protection that outlines principal prevention strategies to address and respond to various forms of child violence and exploitation, including early and forced marriage. On June 24, WILDAF-Benin conducted a public campaign in the village of Sebiohoue in the commune of Djakotomey to raise awareness of early and forced marriage. Local officials and judges participated in the event by addressing the legal implications of early and forced marriage.

<u>Female Genital Mutilation/Cutting (FGM/C)</u>: See information for girls under 18 in women's section above.

<u>Sexual Exploitation of Children</u>: The penal code provides penalties for conviction of rape, sexual exploitation, corruption of minors, and procuring and facilitating prostitution, and it increases penalties for cases involving children under age 15. The child trafficking law provides penalties for conviction of all forms of child trafficking, including child prostitution, prescribing penalties of 10 to 20 years' imprisonment. The act, however, focuses on prohibiting and punishing the movement of children rather than their ultimate exploitation. Individuals convicted of involvement in child prostitution, including those who facilitate and solicit it, face imprisonment of two to five years and fines of one million to 10 million CFA francs ($1,702 to $17,024). The law does not specifically prohibit child pornography. The de facto minimum age for consensual sex is 18.

Children were exploited in prostitution in some areas and subjected to sex trafficking in Cotonou. Commercial sexual exploitation of children occurred. A 2009 report on the commercial sexual exploitation of children in 11 communes indicated that 43 percent of surveyed children (ages 12 to 17) who engaged in prostitution were also subjected to commercial sexual exploitation.

Through the traditional practice of vidomegon, which literally means "placed child," poor, generally rural, children are placed in the home of a wealthier family for educational or vocational opportunities and a higher standard of living; abuse, however, including long hours of forced labor, inadequate food, and sexual exploitation, occurred (see section 7.c.).

Criminal courts meted out stiff sentences to persons convicted of crimes against children, but many such cases never reached the courts due to lack of awareness of the law and children's rights, lack of access to courts, or fear of police involvement.

Infanticide or Infanticide of Children with Disabilities: Despite widespread NGO campaigns, the traditional practices of killing breech babies, babies whose mothers died in childbirth, babies considered deformed, and one of each set of newborn twins (because they were considered sorcerers) continued in the north.

International Child Abductions: The country is not a party to the 1980 Hague Convention on the Civil Aspects of International Child Abduction. See the Department of State's *Annual Report on International Parental Child Abduction* at travel.state.gov/content/childabduction/en/legal/compliance.html.

Anti-Semitism

There was no known Jewish community, and there were no reports of anti-Semitic acts.

Trafficking in Persons

See the Department of State's *Trafficking in Persons Report* at www.state.gov/j/tip/rls/tiprpt/.

Persons with Disabilities

The law does not explicitly prohibit discrimination against persons with physical, sensory, intellectual, or mental disabilities in education, access to health care, or provision of other state services; the law, however, provides that the government care for persons with disabilities. There were no legal requirements for the construction or alteration of buildings to permit access for persons with disabilities. Legislation that addresses equality, equity, and nondiscrimination among all citizens is general in nature. Several laws, however, including the labor code, the social security code, the persons and family code, and the 2011 law establishing general rules for elections, contain specific references to persons with disabilities. The country also has a National Policy for the Protection and Integration of Persons with Disabilities. Children with mental, visual, and physical disabilities, however, suffered social exclusion and had no access to the conventional educational system.

The government operated few institutions to assist persons with disabilities. The Office for the Rehabilitation and the Insertion of Persons with Disabilities under the Ministry of Labor, Civil Service, and Social Affairs coordinated assistance to persons with disabilities through the Aid Fund for the Rehabilitation and Insertion of Persons with Disabilities (Fonds Ariph). An international donor-funded program was conducted by local NGOs to increase awareness of accessibility needs of voters with disabilities in the March presidential election. The program also included the construction of temporary ramps and other adaptations to provide access to polling sites for voters with disabilities.

Acts of Violence, Discrimination, and Other Abuses Based on Sexual Orientation and Gender Identity

There are no laws explicitly criminalizing consensual same-sex sexual activity but such activity could be prosecuted under the public indecency provisions of the penal code. There were no reports of criminal or civil cases involving consensual same-sex sexual conduct or reports of societal discrimination or violence based on a person's sexual orientation. Although homosexual behavior was socially discouraged, it was not prosecuted. A growing number of citizens were open regarding their sexual orientation or gender identity, but the lesbian, gay, bisexual, transgender, and intersex (LGBTI) community remained largely disorganized and hidden. With the support of a regional LGBTI organization, 30 members from Beninese and Togolese LGBTI communities held a conclave in April 2015 in Cotonou to discuss problems pertaining to LGBTI conditions and rights.

Other Societal Violence or Discrimination

Police generally ignored vigilante attacks, and incidents of mob violence occurred, in part due to the perceived failure of local courts to punish criminals adequately. Such cases generally involved mobs killing or severely injuring suspected criminals, particularly thieves caught stealing. On June 18, a mob of Klouekanme residents in the southwestern commune of Couffo burned to death three individuals arrested by gendarmes as part of an investigation to dismantle a criminal ring operating in the area. The mob intercepted the gendarme vehicle transporting the three suspects and dragged them out. From June 24 to June 26, three other similar incidents occurred in the cities of Cotonou, Abomey Calavi, and Djougou. On June 29, the Council of Ministers urged the minister of justice to increase measures to investigate, arrest, and prosecute individuals involved in lynching incidents throughout the country.

Section 7. Worker Rights

a. Freedom of Association and the Right to Collective Bargaining

The law provides for the rights of workers, except certain civil servants and public employees, to form and join independent unions with some restrictions. New unions must register with the Ministry of Interior, a three-month process, or risk a fine. The law does not establish clear grounds on which registration of a trade union may be denied or approved, and official registration may be denied without recourse to an independent court of justice. The law provides that a trade union federation must be made up of at least five enterprise-level trade unions in the same sector or branch of activity. Additionally, the law requires that a trade union confederation must be composed of at least three trade union federations of different sectors or branches of activities; only trade union confederations may have affiliation at a national or international level.

The law provides for the rights of workers to bargain collectively. Collective bargaining agreements are negotiated within a joint committee by law, including representatives of one or several unions and or representatives of one or several employers' associations. A labor inspector, a secretary and one or two rapporteurs, presides over the committee. The minister of labor has the authority to determine which trade unions may be represented in the negotiation at the enterprise level. The minister has the power to extend the scope of coverage of a collective agreement. The law imposes compulsory conciliation and binding arbitration in the event of disputes during collective bargaining in all sectors, "nonessential service" sectors included. The National Permanent Commission for Consultation, the Collective Bargaining Committee, and the Social Sector-based Dialogue Committee were active in each ministry to foster dialogue between the government and unions. The commission, however, did not hold sessions on a regular basis as prescribed by the law, and lacked efficiency. On September 1, the government approved a bill intended to improve the functioning of the commission.

On August 30, the government, the National Employers' Association, and six union confederations signed a "National Charter of Social Dialogue" including several measures to be undertaken by the three parties to enhance dialogue while fostering democracy and good governance in a climate of social accord and national unity.

The law provides for the right to strike, but prior notification must be provided. The merchant marine code grants seafarers the right to organize but not the right to strike. A trade union willing to go on strike should notify (notification letter) its intent to the leadership of the concerned entity, to the minister of civil service or to the minister of labor at least three days before the start of the strike. The notification letter should mention the reasons of the strike, the location, the date, the starting time of the strike and the duration of the strike. Authorities do not actually grant permission to strike, but strikes that fail to comply with these requirements are deemed illegal.

The law provides that civil servants, public- and private-entity workers, and parastatal employees who provide essential services shall maintain minimum services during strikes. The law provides for a discretionary determination of "essential services." It defines essential services as the services pertaining to health, security, energy, water, air transport, and telecommunications. Workers must provide three days' notice before striking and notify authorities of the intended duration of a strike. Authorities may declare strikes illegal for reasons such as threatening social peace and order and may requisition striking workers to maintain minimum services. The government may prohibit any strike on the grounds it threatens the economy or the national interest. Laws prohibit employer retaliation against strikers, except that a company may withhold part of a worker's pay following a strike.

The law prohibits antiunion discrimination and provides for reinstatement of workers fired for union activity. Employers may not take union membership or activity into account in hiring, work distribution, professional or vocational training, or dismissal. In addition to certain civil servants and public employees, domestic workers, agricultural workers, migrant workers, and those in export processing zones are excluded from relevant legal protections.

Workers discussed labor-related issues with employers through the National Consultation and Collective Bargaining Commission. The commission held sessions and met with the government during the year to discuss workers' claims and propose solutions. Information regarding whether or not remedies and penalties had deterrent effects was not available.

The government generally respected the right to form and join independent unions and the right to collective bargaining. With the exception of merchant shipping employees, workers exercised their right to strike. Civil servants went on strike throughout the year. The government did not effectively enforce the law, particularly in the informal sector and with regard to the provisions on antiunion discrimination and reinstatement. There were reports that employers threatened individuals with dismissal for union activity. No violations related to collective bargaining rights were reported.

The Ministry of Foreign Affairs' Union of Diplomats, Interpreters, Translators, Administrative, and Technical Personnel undertook a three-day per week strike from February 16 to March 12. The union demanded better working conditions, the removal from service of individuals who should have statutorily retired, and the return to the Ministry of Foreign Affairs' use a building whose use had been temporarily granted to the Ministry of Civil Service.

b. Prohibition of Forced or Compulsory Labor

The labor code prohibits forced or compulsory labor, with certain exceptions. The law allows for imprisonment with compulsory labor. The law allows authorities to exact work from military conscripts that is not of a purely military character. Laws regulating various acts or activities relating to the exercise of freedom of expression allow imposition of prison sentences involving obligation to perform social rehabilitation work.

Forced labor occurred, including domestic servitude and bonded labor by children. Prosecutions and investigations of trafficking and forced labor decreased from the previous year. Forced labor was mainly found in the agricultural (e.g., cotton and palm oil), artisanal mining, quarrying, fishing, commercial, and construction sectors. Many traffickers were relatives or acquaintances of their victims, exploiting the traditional system of vidomegon, in which parents allow their children to live with and work for richer relatives, usually in urban areas (see section 6).

Also see the Department of State's *Trafficking in Persons Report* at www.state.gov/j/tip/rls/tiprpt/.

c. Prohibition of Child Labor and Minimum Age for Employment

The labor code prohibits the employment or apprenticeship of children under age 14 in any enterprise; children between ages 12 and 14, however, may perform domestic work and temporary or light seasonal work if it does not interfere with their compulsory schooling. The code bans night work for workers under age 18 unless special dispensation is allowed by the government in consultation with the National Labor Council. Workers under age 18 are entitled to a minimum 12-hour uninterrupted break including the nighttime period. The law lists hazardous work activities that are prohibited for children under age 18 and includes 22 trades and 74 related hazardous activities.

The Labor Office, under the Ministry of Labor, Civil Service, and Social Affairs, enforced the labor code only in the formal sector due to a lack of inspectors. The total number of inspections conducted during the year was unavailable. Penalties for those convicted of violating laws were sufficiently strict to serve as a deterrent and ranged from 140,000 CFA francs ($238) to 350,000 CFA francs ($596), sentences of two months to one year in prison, or both.

Labor laws were not effectively enforced. Despite the government's limited capacity to enforce child labor laws, the government continued to take steps to educate parents on the labor code and prevent compulsory labor by children, including through media campaigns, regional workshops, and public pronouncements on child labor problems. These initiatives were part of the Labor Office's traditional sensitization program. The government also worked with a network of NGOs and journalists to educate the population regarding child labor and child trafficking. The Ministries of Justice, and Labor, Family Civil Service, and Social Affairs supported capacity building for officials and agencies responsible for enforcing child labor laws. During the year authorities prosecuted perpetrators of child labor violations in connection with child trafficking. In March 2015 in the city of Parakou in northern Benin, gendarmes arrested an individual suspected of trafficking two underage girls to Kosubosu in Nigeria as domestic laborers. The suspect was reportedly jailed pending further investigation on the charge of involvement in a trafficking network.

To help support their families, children of both sexes, including those as young as age seven, worked on family farms, in small businesses, on construction sites in urban areas, in public markets as street vendors, and as domestic servants under the practice of vidomegon. Under vidomegon many rural parents sent their children to cities to live with relatives or family friends to perform domestic chores in return for receiving an education. Host families did not always honor their part of the arrangement, and abuse and forced labor of child domestic servants was a problem. Children often faced long hours of work, inadequate food, and sexual exploitation--factors indicative of forced labor and exploitation of children in domestic servitude. Sometimes the child's parents and the urban family that raised the child divided between themselves the income generated by the child's activities. Up to

95 percent of children in vidomegon were young girls. Several local NGOs led public education and awareness campaigns to decrease the practice.

A majority of children working as apprentices were under the legal age of 14 for apprenticeship, including children working in construction, car and motorbike repair, hairdressing, and dressmaking. Children worked as laborers with adults in quarries, including crushing granite, in many areas. Children were at times forced to hawk goods and beg, and street children engaged in prostitution (see section 6). Children under age 14 worked in either the formal or informal sectors in the following activities: agriculture, hunting and fishing, industry, construction and public works, trade and vending, food and beverages, transportation, and other services, including employment as household staff.

Children are required to attend only six years of primary school, through age 11. Since the minimum age for children to work is 14, children ages 12 to 13 are particularly vulnerable to the worst forms of child labor, as they may have completed primary school but are not legally permitted to work.

Some parents indentured their children to "agents" recruiting farm hands or domestic workers, often on the understanding that the children's wages would be sent to the parents. In some cases these agents took the children to neighboring countries, including Nigeria, Cote d'Ivoire, Togo, and Ghana, for labor.

Also see the Department of State's *Trafficking in Persons Report* at www.state.gov/j/tip/rls/tiprpt/ and the Department of Labor's *Findings on the Worst Forms of Child Labor* at www.dol.gov/ilab/reports/child-labor/findings/.

d. Discrimination with Respect to Employment and Occupation

The constitution and labor code prohibit discrimination with respect to employment and occupation based on race, color, sex, religion, political opinion, national origin or citizenship, social origin, and disability. The laws, however, do not explicitly prohibit discrimination based on sexual orientation, gender identity, and HIV-positive status or other communicable diseases. The government, in general, effectively enforced these laws and regulations in most sectors. Women experienced extensive discrimination because of societal attitudes and resistance to behavioral change (see section 6). Women's wages consistently lagged behind those of men. Employment discrimination occurred in the private and public sectors. According to the National Institute of Statistics and Economic Analysis, the employment rate was 73 percent for men and 69 percent for women in 2011. The prohibitions on discrimination did not apply to the large informal sector.

The labor code includes provisions to protect the employment rights of workers with disabilities, which were enforced with limited effectiveness.

The Office of Labor under the Ministry of Labor, Civil Service, and Social Affairs is responsible for protecting the rights of persons with disabilities.

Migrant workers enjoyed the same legal protections, wages, and working conditions as citizens.

e. Acceptable Conditions of Work

The government set minimum wage scales for a number of occupations. In 2014 the government increased the minimum wage to 40,000 CFA francs ($68) per month from 30,000 CFA francs ($51) per month.

The labor code establishes a workweek of between 40 and 46 hours, depending on the type of work, and provides for at least one 24-hour rest period per week. Domestic and agricultural workers frequently worked 70 hours or more per week, above the maximum provided for under the labor code of 12 hours per day or 60 hours per week. The labor code also mandates premium pay for overtime and prohibits excessive compulsory overtime.

The law establishes occupational safety and health standards (OSH). The government has the authority to require employers to remedy dangerous work conditions but did not effectively do so. Provisions of the law related to acceptable conditions of work apply to all workers. Penalties for violating the labor code were not sufficient to deter violations. On September 6, the first annual session of Benin's National Labor Council focused on proper enforcement of the minimum wage by the government and private sector employers.

The Ministry of Labor, Civil Service, and Social Affairs was responsible for enforcement of the minimum wage, workweek, and OSH standards. The ministry did not effectively enforce these standards, especially in the large informal sector. Significant parts of the work force and foreign migrant workers did not benefit, in practice, from minimum wage scales. Authorities generally enforced legal limits on workweeks in the formal sector but did not effectively monitor or control foreign or migrant workers' conditions of work. Government efforts were impeded by the small number of labor inspectors and lack of resources to implement inspections. There were 75 labor officers, composed of 56 labor inspectors, 15 administrators, and four labor controllers. Random inspections were conducted in some sectors during the year, but no information was available on the number of violations or convictions. The government took unsuccessful measures to deter persons from engaging in the sale of smuggled gasoline from Nigeria. The government supported informal workers by granting them credits to expand their businesses as part of its microcredit project for the poor.

Many workers supplemented their wages by subsistence farming or informal sector trade. Most workers in the formal sector earned more than the minimum wage; many domestic and other laborers in the informal sector earned less. Violations of OSH standards mostly occurred in informal-sector trades, including hairdressing, dressmaking, baking, mechanics, and carpentry, where workers faced biological, chemical, physical, and psychological risks. Children involved in these trades as apprentices worked long hours and were more vulnerable to hazardous working conditions. In some of the mechanic and carpentry shops, children worked alongside adults while the adults used various tools and equipment, and some adults and children lacked adequate protective gear. According to various sources, informal workers accounted for more than 90 percent of the total number of workers in the country. Informal workers faced numerous challenges and vulnerabilities, including long working hours and no social security coverage. They often endured substandard working conditions and were exposed to occupational risks. No data on workplace fatalities and accidents was available.

The law does not provide workers with the right to remove themselves from dangerous work situations without jeopardy to continued employment.

www.ingramcontent.com/pod-product-compliance
Lightning Source LLC
Chambersburg PA
CBHW081258250726
48654CB00012B/1649